The MAILBOX®

Preschool

Let's PLAY

Y0-CAG-951

Play-based learning activities for **22** everyday themes!

- Encourage active exploration
- Spark natural curiosity
- Increase problem solving and reasoning
- Make learning fun

Managing Editor: Kimberly Ann Brugger

Editorial Team: Becky S. Andrews, Diane Badden, Tricia Kylene Brown, Kimberley Bruck, Karen A. Brudnak, Julie Christensen, Elizabeth Cook, Pam Crane, Chris Curry, Roxanne LaBell Dearman, Brenda Fay, Pierce Foster, Ada H. Goren, Tazmen Hansen, Marsha Heim, Lori Z. Henry, Debra Liverman, Kitty Lowrance, Desiree Magnani, Toni-Ann Maisano, Tina Petersen, Mark Rainey, Greg D. Rieves, Hope Rodgers-Medina, Rebecca Saunders, Donna K. Teal, Sharon M. Tresino, Zane Williard

www.themailbox.com

©2012 The Mailbox® Books
All rights reserved.
ISBN 978-1-61276-163-3

Printed in the United States
10 9 8 7 6 5 4 3 2 1

HPS 233454

Table of Contents

What's Inside

22 themes

167 play-based activities

Ideas for independent play

Ideas for teacher-guided play

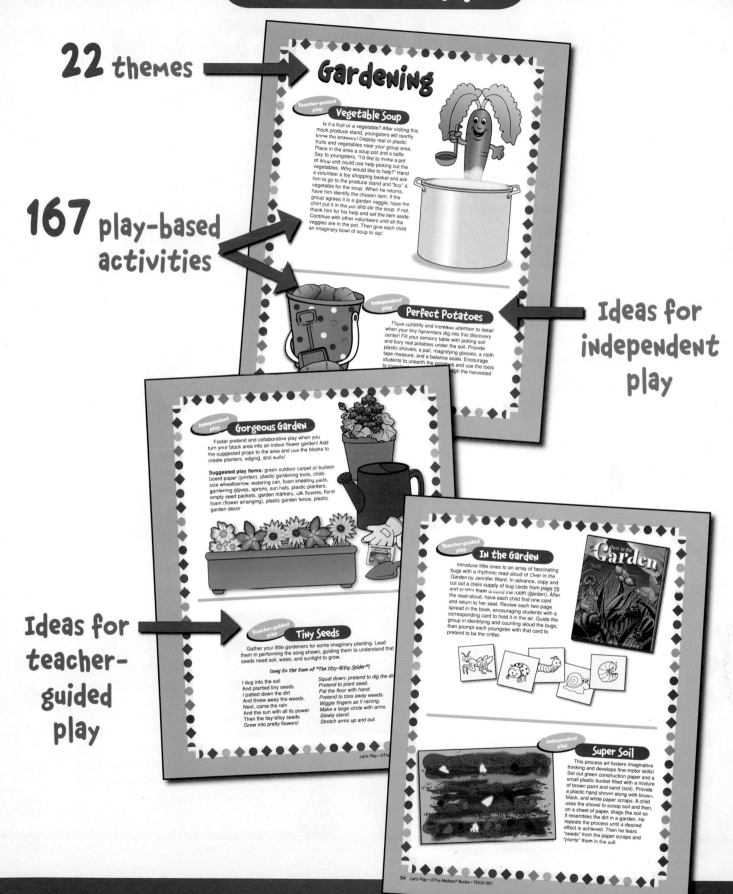

Gardening

Vegetable Soup
Teacher-guided play

Is it a fruit or a vegetable? After visiting this mock produce stand, youngsters will readily know the answers! Display real or plastic fruits and vegetables near your group area. Place in the area a soup pot and a ladle. Say to youngsters, "I'd like to make a pot of soup and could use help picking out the vegetables. Who would like to help?" Hand a volunteer a toy shopping basket and ask him to go to the produce stand and "buy" a vegetable for the soup. When he returns, have him identify the chosen item. If the group agrees it is a garden veggie, have the child put it in the pot and stir the soup. If not, thank him for his help and set the item aside. Continue with other volunteers until all the veggies are in the pot. Then give each child an imaginary bowl of soup to sip!

Perfect Potatoes
Independent play

Pique curiosity and increase attention to detail when your tiny harvesters dig into this discovery center! Fill your sensory table with potting soil and bury real potatoes under the soil. Provide plastic shovels, a pail, magnifying glasses, a cloth tape measure, and a balance scale. Encourage students to unearth the potatoes and use the tools to investigate... weigh the harvested...

Gorgeous Garden
Independent play

Foster pretend and collaborative play when you turn your block area into an indoor flower garden! Add the suggested props to the area and use the blocks to create planters, edging, and walls!

Suggested play items: green outdoor carpet or bulletin board paper (garden), plastic gardening tools, child-size wheelbarrow, watering can, foam kneeling pads, gardening gloves, aprons, sun hats, plastic planters, empty seed packets, garden markers, silk flowers, floral foam (flower arranging), plastic garden fence, plastic garden decor

Tiny Seeds
Teacher-guided play

Gather your little gardeners for some imaginary planting. Lead them in performing the song shown, guiding them to understand that seeds need soil, water, and sunlight to grow.

(sung to the tune of "The Itsy-Bitsy Spider")

I dug into the soil
And planted tiny seeds.
I patted down the dirt
And threw away the weeds.
Next, came the rain
And the sun with all its power.
Then the itsy-bitsy seeds
Grew into pretty flowers!

Squat down; pretend to dig the dir...
Pretend to plant seed.
Pat the floor with hand.
Pretend to toss away weeds.
Wiggle fingers as if raining.
Make a large circle with arms.
Slowly stand.
Stretch arms up and out.

Let's Play • ©The...

In the Garden
Teacher-guided play

Introduce little ones to an array of fascinating bugs with a rhythmic read-aloud of *Over in the Garden* by Jennifer Ward. In advance, copy and cut out a class supply of bug cards from page 55 and scatter them around the room (garden). After the read-aloud, have each child find one card and return to her seat. Review each two-page spread in the book, encouraging students with a corresponding card to hold it in the air. Guide the group in identifying and counting aloud the bugs; then prompt each youngster with that card to pretend to be the critter.

Super Soil
Independent play

This process art fosters imaginative thinking and develops fine-motor skills! Set out green construction paper and a small plastic bucket filled with a mixture of brown paint and sand (soil). Provide a plastic hand shovel along with brown, black, and white paper scraps. A child uses the shovel to scoop soil and then, on a sheet of paper, drags the soil so it resembles the dirt in a garden. He repeats the process until a desired effect is achieved. Then he tears "seeds" from the paper scraps and "plants" them in the soil.

Around the Town

Bake a Cake

Here's a playful idea that gives little ones a fine-motor workout and encourages speaking skills! Gather a small group of students and teach them the traditional rhyme "Patty-Cake." Then give each child a copy of the cake pattern on page 7 and provide a variety of collage materials. Have students pretend to be bakers as they decorate their cakes. As they decorate, ask them questions such as the following: Who is this cake for? What flavor is your cake going to be? What is your favorite dessert?

Fix It!

This idea is packed with role-playing fun! Place a variety of play tools near a table (car). Also provide rags for wiping grease and a scooter board, if desired. A child gets on his back on the scooter board and scoots beneath the car to "fix" it.

Wait Staff

Give youngsters balancing practice as they pretend to be waiters or waitresses. Provide several disposable bowls and cups as well as a tray. You can even provide plastic food! A child places food in the bowls and cups and then puts them on the tray. Next, she attempts to hold the tray on her palm. When she has the tray balanced, she tries walking around the room.

Construction Time!

Little ones pretend to be construction workers when they perform this action-packed song! Guide little ones in singing the song and enthusiastically pantomiming each verse.

(sung to the tune of "The Mulberry Bush")

This is the way we [hammer a nail, hammer a nail, hammer a nail].
This is the way we [hammer a nail]
When it's construction time!

Continue with the following: *saw a board, tighten a screw, climb a ladder, pull with pliers*

Hot Pot!

Little ones pretend to be chefs with this writing activity! Write "Preschool Soup" on a sheet of chart paper and place a soup pot nearby. Next, ask a little chef what he wants to put in the soup. Write his ingredient on the chart paper. Then have him pretend to chop up his ingredient and place it in the pot. Prompt little ones to say "Splash!" as he drops it in. Continue with each remaining youngster. Then have everyone pretend to taste the soup!

Preschool Soup
chicken
macaroni and cheese
2 slices of pizza
tomatoes
chocolate cookies

Sanitation Situation

Spotlight sanitation engineers with this active role-playing idea! Place small empty trash cans around the room. Then arrange several chairs to make a pretend garbage truck. Provide gloves, a disposable plate (steering wheel), and a key ring (keys to the truck). Youngsters use the items to role-play collecting the garbage and driving the truck.

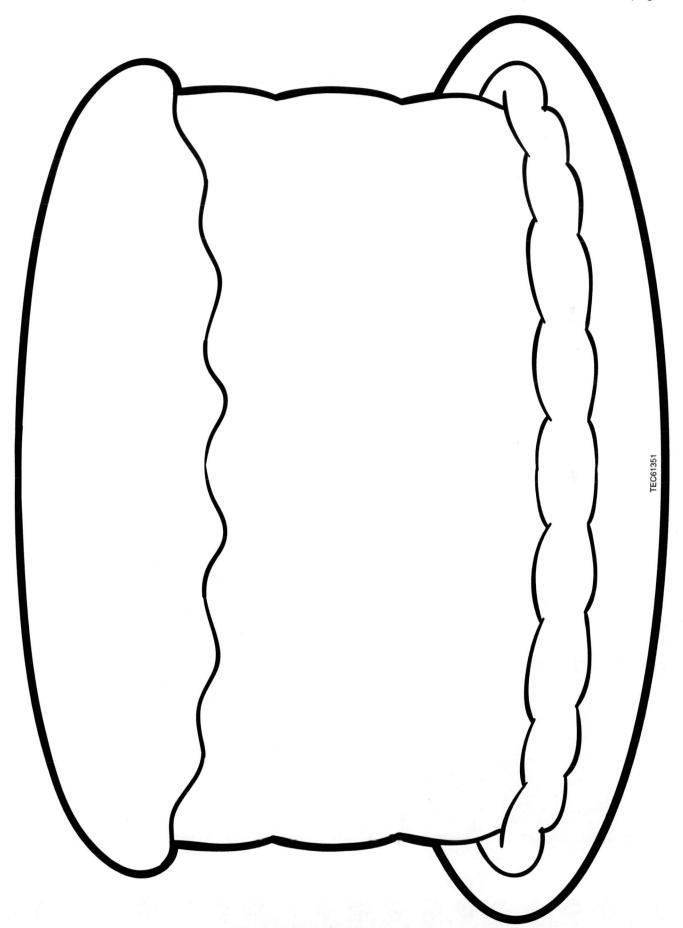

TEC61351

Beach

Beach Ball Blast

Partner play is the key to success in this fun beach ball game! Invite two players to hold the opposite ends of a beach towel. Toss a beach ball toward the youngsters and encourage them to catch it with the towel. Then, on the count of three, have them fling the ball back to you using the towel.

Flip-Flop Drop

Playfully engage youngsters in matching pairs of summer footwear! Collect pairs of flip-flops in different colors or designs. Place one flip-flop from each pair in a beach bag. Gather a small group of youngsters and seat them in a circle. Then give each child one of the remaining flip-flops. Tell little ones you need help matching their flip-flops to ones that are in the beach bag. Then have them chant "Flip-flop drop!" As they say the word *drop*, toss a flip-flop from the bag into the middle of the circle. Encourage each child to scan the footwear and retrieve it if they have the matching flip-flop. Continue until all the flip-flops are paired.

Super Sandcastles

Creative sand-castle construction provides a fantastic fine-motor workout! Knead sand into brown play dough. Then place the mixture at a table along with a plastic ice cube tray (for making play dough cubes to build sand-castle walls) and a plastic knife (to remove the cubes from the tray). Also provide items such as medium-size seashells, construction paper flags, rocks, and small craft feathers.

Seaside Ditty

Little ones pack for an imaginary trip to the beach! Present a beach bag and a variety of items one might pack for the beach, such as sunglasses, sunscreen, flip-flops, a beach towel, shorts, a T-shirt, and beach toys. Have a child choose an item and say, "I'm going to pack [item name]!" Encourage her to place it in the bag and then lead students in singing the song shown. Continue until all the items are packed, singing the song between each addition.

(sung to the tune of "The Farmer in the Dell")

I'm packing for the beach!
I'm packing for the beach!
Sand, sun, and lots of fun,
I'm packing for the beach!

Fun at the Beach

Inspire pretend play and encourage social interaction with an indoor beach getaway! Simply stage an open area of the room with the suggested items. To enhance the playful atmosphere, put on a recording of summertime music.

Suggested play items: blue bed sheet or blanket (water); beach towels; beach bags; clean, empty sunscreen bottles; sunglasses; swim goggles; cooler with play food; child-size beach chairs; large seashells; summer-related books; beach hats

Fun at the Beach

Don't Forget the Sunscreen!

Putting on sunscreen will be a breeze after this fun fingerpainting experience! Give each student a skin-tone child cutout (see pattern on page 11). Provide white paint (sunscreen) and crayons. Encourage her to draw a swimsuit and other desired details on the cutout. Then have her apply sunscreen to the exposed parts of the body. Remind her to be careful not to get sunscreen in the child's eyes! As the youngster works, discuss with her why it's important to wear sunscreen. If desired, display the cutouts on a board with beach-related details and the title "We're Ready for the Sun!"

TEC61351

Bugs

Dance, Beetles, Dance!

Give young bug aficionados a sneak peek at the fascinating world of beetles with a read-aloud of *Beetle Bop* by Denise Fleming. After sharing the book, ask youngsters to pretend they are beetles. Then call out commands—such as "Fly, beetles, fly!" or "Crawl, beetles, crawl!"—for your little beetles to follow, taking inspiration from the busy beetles throughout the book. Periodically call out "Beetle bop!" and play lively dance music while your little beetles dance!

Independent play

Interesting Insects

Incorporate some insect insight into your play dough center and watch youngsters go buggy for bugs! Provide a nonfiction book or magazine that shows the different body parts of many bugs. Also provide play dough, pipe cleaner pieces, snippets of plastic straws, and wings cut from laminating film. Encourage youngsters to use the bug reference as inspiration for creating insects with the materials provided.

Flight of the Bumblebees

Ever heard of bees that fly, buzz, and count? Well, that's what they do in this playful game! Place two oversize beehive cutouts on the floor. Prompt your little bumblebees to "fly" around the room, making buzzing sounds as they go. After a few moments, dim the lights and prompt the bees to fly to either hive. After all the bees have "landed," lead them in counting how many are in each hive. Help students determine which hive has more bees, which hive has fewer bees, or if the number of bees in the hives are equal. Then turn up the lights and repeat the activity.

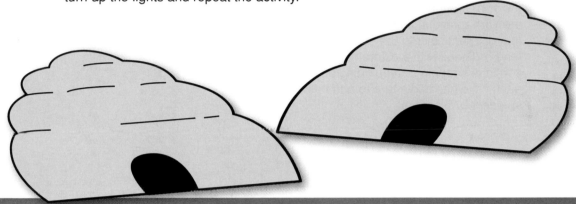

Bugs, Bugs, and More Bugs!

What happens when you turn your sensory table into an insect haven? Youngsters get a fine-motor workout and develop sorting skills! Fill the table with green paper shreds (grass). Then hide a collection of two or more distinctly different types of plastic or craft foam bugs in the grass. Provide a bug box (or plastic container with holes poked in the lid) for each type of bug, plastic tweezers, and magnifying glasses. Little ones use the magnifying glasses to search for bugs and the tweezers to sort them in the bug boxes.

Big Beautiful Web!

Youngsters make a lovely colorful web with this playful activity! Cut notches in a large square cardboard panel and attach the end of a length of yarn to it. Then invite a child to wrap the yarn around the cardboard. When the yarn runs out, tie a length of yarn in a different color to the end of the first length. Then invite a different child to continue wrapping. Keep going until each child has had a turn to add to the spiderweb. What fun!

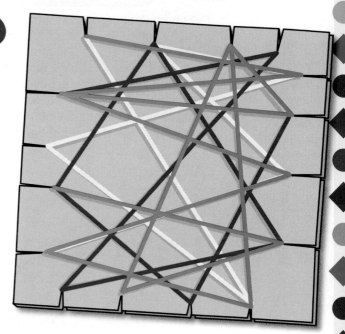

There's a Bug on My...

Who would have thought that creepy-crawly critters could be so instrumental in practicing body-parts awareness! Give each child a plastic bug. Then lead youngsters in singing the song, prompting students to place their insects on the appropriate body part as they sing. Repeat the song, substituting other body parts.

(sung to the tune of "If You're Happy and You Know It")

There's a bug on my [head], on my [head]!
There's a bug on my [head], on my [head]!
Oh, it gave me quite a scare.
I don't think I like it there!
There's a bug on my [head], on my [head]!

Ladybug Spots

How many spots does a ladybug have? With this counting game, the number of spots varies round to round! You will need an oversize oval of red felt, ten black felt circles (spots), and number cards labeled from 1 to 10. Invite a child to pretend she's a ladybug and drape the red felt over her back. Then display a card and have the group identify the number. Invite a student to put that many spots on the ladybug's back. Encourage his classmates to count each spot aloud as he works. After confirming that the ladybug has the correct number of spots, invite her to crawl to a classmate, who then becomes the next ladybug.

Caterpillar Crawl

Stimulate imaginations in your art area with pretend caterpillar play! Set out large construction paper leaves, a shallow container of paint, and lengths of thick yarn. A youngster dips a length of yarn in paint and then, pretending the yarn is a crawling caterpillar, moves it around on a leaf. He repeats the process several times before arranging the caterpillar on the leaf to dry.

Camping

Let's Build a Campfire!

Engage critical-thinking skills when you ask your little campers about campfire safety. Provide rocks, cardboard tubes (logs), and orange tissue paper (flames). Review the items with youngsters. Then ask, "What might the rocks be used for?" Encourage students to share their thoughts, leading them to understand that building a ring of rocks helps to contain a campfire and prevent forest fires. Ask other campfire safety questions, such as "Should you ever walk away from a campfire and leave it burning?" and "How could someone put out a campfire when it's no longer needed?" Finally, have students help you build a mock campfire; then turn down the lights and read a camping-related story to the group. Don't forget to have little ones "put out the fire" when you're done!

Cozy Campsite

Give youngsters a preview of what it's like to go camping without actually being in the wilderness! Create a makeshift campsite in your classroom using the suggested items shown.

Suggested play items: small dome tent, sleeping bags, backpacks, child-size outdoor chairs, canteens, a cooler, play food, cookware, utensils, plates, first-aid kit (with bandages, gauze, and first-aid tape), rain ponchos, flashlights, binoculars, compass, toy fishing poles and fish cutouts, mock campfire *(See campfire activity above.)*

Homemade Trail Mix

Invite your little campers to help prepare a batch of tasty camping treats! Provide finger foods, such as cereal, fish-shaped crackers, pretzels, chow mein noodles, and M&M's Minis candies. Encourage each child to scoop a small portion of each ingredient into a large bowl and gently mix it with a wooden spoon. As children work, ask them to share their thoughts about foods that would and would not be good to bring on a camping trip and explain why. After all the ingredients are mixed together, help each child scoop a portion of the trail mix into an individual resealable plastic bag. Then invite youngsters to nibble on their treats.

Mosquitoes!

Gather little ones for this adorable song about a not-so-adorable critter! Have half the youngsters pretend to be buzzing mosquitoes and the remaining students pretend to be campers in their sleeping bags. Lead the campers in singing the song as the mosquitoes buzz around. Then during the final line of the song, encourage them to pretend to spray mosquito spray. Prompt the mosquitoes to gently fall to the floor and cease buzzing.

(sung to the tune of "The Muffin Man")

Buzz, buzz, buzz—mosquitoes buzz.
Mosquitoes buzz; mosquitoes buzz.
Buzz, buzz, buzz—mosquitoes buzz
As I lay in my tent.

Time to get mosquito spray,
Mosquito spray, mosquito spray.
Time to get mosquito spray
And spray it—shhhh, shhhh, shhhh!

Invent a Tent

Inspire collaborative play and critical-thinking skills when you invite little ones to design their own tents! Provide tent-making materials—such as bedsheets, blankets, or small tarps—for youngsters to drape over chairs, tables, or bookcases. To hold the tent edges down, provide items such as blocks, phone books, or socks filled with rice or beans and secured with a knot. Have available a few camping supplies and camping-related books for youngsters to use in their tents!

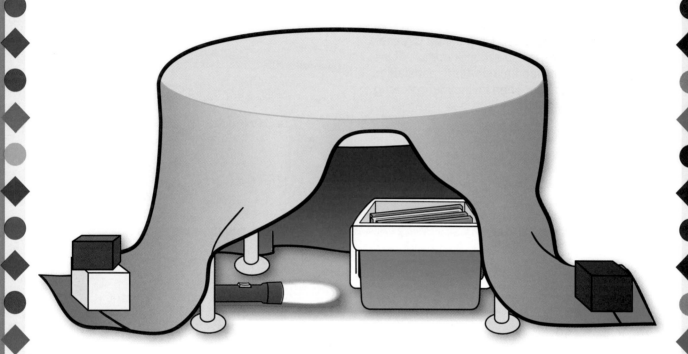

Whoooo! Whoooo!

Whoooo! Whoooo!

Perk up youngsters' listening ears with a familiar woodland sound! Invite a child (camper) to sit with her back to the group. Silently choose a classmate to be the owl. Lead the class in saying, "I see an owl up in the tree!" Then immediately prompt the owl to say, "Whoooo! Whoooo!" Encourage the camper to guess the owl within a predetermined number of guesses. After the owl is guessed or revealed, he becomes the next camper.

Animal Tracks

Enliven imaginations as your little campers create trails of woodland animal tracks! Provide paper, shallow containers of paint, and sponges trimmed so they resemble animal hoof, foot, or paw prints. Invite each child to dip a sponge in paint and press it on a sheet of paper. Have him repeat the process several times to create trails of animal tracks. As youngsters work, encourage them to tell stories about the animals that made the tracks and what happened along their journeys. Record each child's dictation and attach it to his page.

Digging for Bait

Avid campers know that camping and fishing go hand-in-hand! Provide youngsters with loads of sensory fun by having them dig for worms. Fill your sensory table or a large plastic tub with potting soil. Bury rubber worms (found in sporting goods stores) or pieces of large rubber bands in the soil. Provide a plastic shovel and pail. A child digs for worms and then places them in the pail.

Construction

On the Job

Direct your little construction workers to "punch in" on an imaginary time clock and head off to the construction site (group area). Then lead youngsters in performing this fun action song!

(sung to the tune of "Shoo Fly")

Hammers go up and down.   *Move up and down.*
Hammers go up and down.
Hammers go up and down.
Whack, whack, whack and pound, pound, pound!

Screwdrivers go left and right.   *Twist body from left to right.*
Screwdrivers go left and right.
Screwdrivers go left and right.
Make it loose or make it tight!

Handsaws go front and back.   *Lean forward and backward.*
Handsaws go front and back.
Handsaws go front and back.
Pile those boards up in a stack!

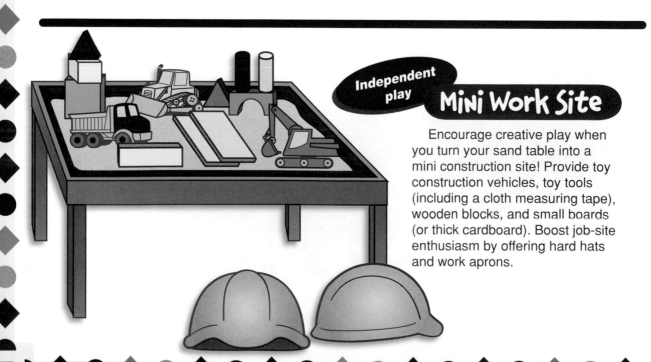

Independent play

Mini Work Site

Encourage creative play when you turn your sand table into a mini construction site! Provide toy construction vehicles, toy tools (including a cloth measuring tape), wooden blocks, and small boards (or thick cardboard). Boost job-site enthusiasm by offering hard hats and work aprons.

Pint-Size Painters

What happens to water after painting with it? Inspire your pint-size painters to discover the answer with this water-based painting activity! Provide buckets of water, paintbrushes, paint trays with water, and paint rollers. If desired, provide painters' caps as well! Take youngsters outside and invite them to use the water and tools to "paint" sidewalks, walls, or pavement in direct sunlight and in shade. As they work, guide students to talk about their observations of the water during and after painting, leading them to understand that the water evaporates. Encourage youngsters to compare evaporation of water in the sun and in the shade.

Nail It!

Build hand-eye coordination and muscle strength with hammering! Cover a tabletop with butcher paper and set out construction paper rectangles (boards), shallow containers of paint, hole reinforcers or sticky dots, and a toy hammer. Make sure to provide paint smocks! Invite a child to press several sticky dots on a board, carefully marking where to hammer. Then have him dip the hammer in paint and pound it on a dot. If desired, encourage him to hammer using other colors of paint, guiding him to notice color blending and unique splatter designs.

Cool Construction

Build creativity and critical-thinking skills when you transform your block area into a construction zone! Simply add the suggested items shown to your existing building blocks.

Suggested play items: empty boxes and containers, sheets of thick cardboard (foundations), cardboard tubes, plastic piping (plumbing), toy tools and toolbox, measuring devices, authentic level, hard hats, traffic cones, safety glasses, first aid kit, paper and crayons (signs, blueprints), paint trays, paint rollers, paintbrushes

Brilliant Blueprints!

Give little ones a bird's-eye view of what it takes to build a house with a read-aloud of *Building a House* by Byron Barton. Ask students to recall the various professionals involved in building a house, emphasizing that an architect draws the blueprints, or detailed plans, for building a structure. Then provide blue paper and white crayons and encourage your little architects to draw blueprints of their own! When the blueprints are finalized, invite youngsters to take them to the block area and build a model of the plans.

Movin' Materials

How do building materials get to the job site? How do construction workers move the materials? Youngsters explore these challenges with some engaging pretend play! Provide supplies to be hauled, such as wooden blocks, building logs, rocks, cardboard tubes, and thread spools. Also provide large toy construction vehicles and equipment like dump trucks, bulldozers, cranes, and a wheelbarrow. When the hauling is done, youngsters clean up the job site and store the cargo!

Foreman Says...

Incorporate play into a familiar game with a construction-themed twist! Have youngsters slowly spin around like a cement mixer, rapidly jump up and down like a jackhammer, and extend their arms and move them from side to side like a crane. After practicing the movements, pretend to be a construction-site foreman and call out job orders such as "Foreman says to use the crane," "Foreman says to mix cement," and "Foreman says to use the jackhammer." After several rounds, say, "Foreman says to take a break," prompting youngsters to sit down. Then say, "Foreman says to get back to work," prompting students to stand and listen for further instructions.

Foreman says to use the jackhammer.

Dinosaurs

Here Comes T. rex!

Invite youngsters to join you for an imaginary encounter with *T. rex*! Lead little ones in singing the song and performing the suggested motions.

(sung to the tune of "Are You Sleeping?")

Here comes *T. rex*,
Here comes *T. rex*,
On the prowl.
Hear him growl.
Hear his heavy footsteps
Stomping oh so loudly.
Run away!
Run away!

Hold fingers like claws.
Slowly walk around.

Pretend to growl like a dinosaur.
Stomp feet.

Run in place.

Independent play

Prehistoric Prints

Entice youngsters with a process art activity that has a prehistoric twist! Provide plastic dinosaurs, paper, shallow containers of paint, and sand. A child dips a dinosaur's feet in paint and then "stomps" the dinosaur on a sheet of paper, adding more paint to the feet as needed. As he stomps the dinosaur, he says, "Roar!" Then he sprinkles a dusting of sand onto the wet footprints.

Meat or Plant Platter?

Little ones sharpen scissor skills when they prepare a delectable dinosaur dinner! Set out paper plates, grocery store circulars and catalogs with meat and plant pictures, scissors, and glue sticks. Explain to students that some dinosaurs are meat eaters and some are plant eaters. Then invite each child to prepare a delicious dinner for a dinosaur by cutting out pictures and gluing them to a plate. As she works, prompt her to consider her food choices by asking, "What type of dinosaur do you think would like this dinner: a plant eater or a meat eater?"

Dino Play!

Youngsters use their imaginations and fine-motor skills when they create dinosaurs! Set out play dough, dinosaur cookie cutters, and items like pasta, pipe cleaner pieces, and sequins to use as scales, claws, and horns. Also provide accessories such as plastic trees, twigs, and medium-size rocks and encourage youngsters to engage in pretend dinosaur play with their prehistoric creations.

Independent play

Dinosaur Dig

Inspire paleontology play by turning your sand table into a dinosaur dig! Simply bury items in the sand and provide the tools mentioned.

Suggested play items: plastic dinosaurs, craft foam dinosaur teeth and bones, pasta noodles (dinosaur claws), medium-size rocks, plastic shovels, sifters, tweezers, chubby paintbrushes (to brush sand from excavated specimens), tray (for collecting findings)

Independent play

Dino Land

Imaginations will soar when you transform your block area into a prehistoric dinosaur den! Provide the suggested items shown and watch the creative play flourish!

Suggested play items: assortment of plastic and stuffed toy dinosaurs, artificial plants, silk leaves, medium-size rocks, twigs, blue bulletin board paper (body of water)

Teacher-guided play

"Egg-cellent" Sorting

Youngsters can hunt and sort dinosaur eggs right in the classroom! Scatter egg cutouts (or plastic eggs) in three different colors around the room. Then tell little ones that they need to collect the dinosaur eggs, but they must be very quiet so they don't wake the dinosaurs. Encourage students to tiptoe as they collect eggs and bring them to a designated spot. Next, help students sort the eggs. When the sorting is finished, have them each take an egg and tiptoe to return it before the dinosaurs notice it's missing.

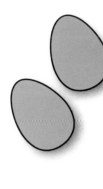

Teacher-guided play

Outstanding Opposites

Introduce youngsters to the wonderful world of opposites through the rollicking, rhyming text of Paul Strickland's *Dinosaur Roar!* Following a read-aloud of the book, engage little ones in some dinosaur antics done opposite-style. Ask youngsters to pretend they are dinosaurs. Then review the pages of the book with your little dinosaurs, guiding them in performing appropriate actions for the opposites on each spread.

Roar really loud. Now make a tiny squeak.

DINOSAUR ROAR!

• PAUL & HENRIETTA STICKLAND •

Earth

Preschool Prospectors

Strengthen fine-motor and sorting skills when you turn your sensory table into a gold mine! Fill the table with sand. Bury in the sand a collection of rocks, most of them painted gold (gold nuggets). (Hint: spray-painting the rocks is fast and economical.) Also provide plastic shovels, sifters, and a bucket for collecting the gold nuggets. For added fun, provide your preschool prospectors with hard hats and safety goggles.

Splash!

Help youngsters learn the difference between rivers and lakes with this simple and playful action song!

(sung to the tune of "Did You Ever See a Lassie?")

Did you ever see a river, a river, a river?   *Move hands like a meandering river.*
Did you ever see a river go this way and that?
It babbles and rushes, and it never hushes.
Did you ever see a river go this way and that?

Did you ever see a lake, a lake, a lake?   *Hold out arms to make a circle.*
Did you ever see a lake, so quiet and still?
It can be quite glassy or wavy and splashy.
Did you ever see a lake, so quiet and still?

Rock and Roll

Preschoolers build auditory skills when they shake, rattle, and roll these easy-to-make shakers! Put small rocks in several different recyclable containers, such as a plastic jar, a coffee can, a margarine tub, and an oatmeal container. Secure each lid with heavy-duty tape. Invite your little music makers to manipulate the shakers, encouraging them to listen to and compare the sounds.

Watch the Water!

Youngsters make stone soup with this fun science investigation! Partially fill a clear container (soup pot) with water (soup). Mark the soup level with a marker or masking tape. Also provide a collection of medium-size rocks and a large mixing spoon. Begin by directing youngsters' attention to the soup level. Then invite your little soup chefs to take turns adding stones to the pot and stirring the soup. Encourage youngsters to observe and describe what happens to the soup level as more stones are added. After determining that the soup level rises, ask, "What do you think would happen if we removed the stones?" To conclude the activity, remove the stones, one at a time, and encourage youngsters to describe what happens.

Skyscape

Boost visual discrimination skills when you invite youngsters to create a billowy skyscape filled with familiar shapes. Trace assorted shapes onto light blue bulletin board paper. Place the paper on a tabletop and provide glue sticks and a supply of cotton balls or loose batting. A youngster identifies a shape and then uses a glue stick and cotton to fill in the outline. Wow! That cloud looks just like a rabbit!

Teacher-guided play

Muddy Fingers

Tantalize fingertips with this discovery-based art experience! Give each child a bowl of potting soil and encourage him to observe, feel, and describe the soil. Then have him pour water onto the soil and stir it with a plastic spoon. Guide him in talking about changes he observes and feels in the mixture, using words such as *dry, wet, thick, thin, thicker, thinner, muddy,* and *lumpy.* Finally, invite him to use a paintbrush to paint his paper with the mixture. As he paints, encourage him to name things he might find in mud. If desired, provide items such as stones, twigs, grass, and yarn pieces (worms) to glue to his artwork.

Fabulous Fossils

Develop visual discrimination and fine-motor skills when you inspire your little researchers to make fossils! Provide self-hardening clay along with items such as small toy dinosaurs, plastic fish, shells, silk leaves, and twigs. Explain that many fossils are impressions made by plant or animal remains and that most fossils are formed when the remains are buried in mud or sand that eventually turns to rock. Invite each child to make impressions in a lump of clay using the provided items; then set his favorite impression aside to harden. After the clay has hardened, encourage youngsters to examine the impressions and guess what made them.

Marvelous Mud

Invite your little dessert chefs to try their hands at making a tasty mud recipe! Elicit youngsters' help in preparing a class-size portion of instant chocolate pudding (mud). Then have each child spoon some of the prepared mud into a clear plastic cup. Next, give each youngster a chocolate cookie sealed inside a resealable plastic bag. Have her cover the bag with a cloth and then crush the cookie by gently tapping it with a clean rock until the cookie resembles dirt. Have her sprinkle the dirt atop the mud and mix it with a spoon. Then invite little ones to eat their marvelously muddy treats!

Fairy Tales and More

Teacher-guided play

Musical Review

Engage little ones in a musical review of the story events in *The Little Red Hen.* Lead youngsters in singing the song and performing appropriate actions.

(sung to the tune of "Mary Had a Little Lamb")

Little Red Hen [planted wheat],
[Planted wheat, planted wheat].
Little Red Hen [planted wheat]—
She did it all alone!

Continue with the following:
cut the wheat, ground the wheat, baked the bread, ate the bread

Independent play

Baking Bread

Encourage role-playing and collaboration after reading aloud a favorite version of *The Little Red Hen.* Add the suggested items to your dramatic-play area, and watch the bread making begin!

Suggested play items: mixing bowls and spoons, measuring cups, plastic eggs, milk and flour containers, bread pans, clean margarine tubs, plastic jelly jars, toy (or craft foam) bread slices, aprons, oven mitts, paper plates, plastic knives, brown play dough

Cross the Bridge

With this simple setting, little ones will be eager to act as the billy goats from *The Three Billy Goats Gruff*! Place in your block area a sheet of blue bulletin board paper (river). Encourage youngsters to build a block bridge across the river and then act out how each goat outsmarts the hungry troll!

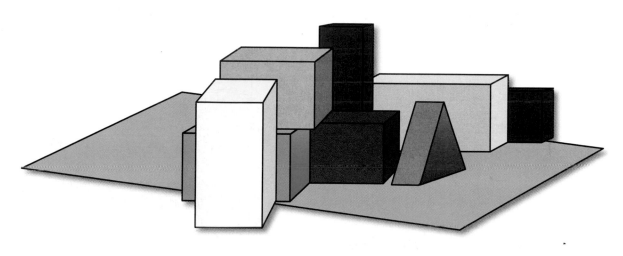

Trip, Trap...Splash!

Youngsters practice a new gross-motor move Billy Goat Gruff–style! Review with youngsters how the big billy goat butted the troll into the river using his head and horns. Then display an inflated balloon programmed with a troll-like face and invite a child to play the part of big Billy Goat Gruff. Have the goat stamp his feet as if he's crossing the bridge, prompting youngsters to say, "Trip, trap, trip, trap." Then toss the troll toward the goat and have him deflect it with his head. When he butts the troll away, prompt the group to say "Splash!" as if the troll fell into the river. After each child gets a chance to play, deflate the balloon and throw it away in a secure area.

Building Houses

After a read-aloud of the classic tale *The Three Little Pigs*, invite little ones to try making houses that are similar to those in the story. Provide red paper rectangles (bricks), craft sticks (sticks), and yellow paper strips (straw) at a table. Provide cardboard boxes and glue. Encourage youngsters to make houses of bricks, sticks, and straw. Then prompt little ones to use the houses for imaginary play with pig and wolf toys.

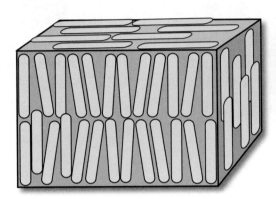

Huff and Puff

What's the benefit of imitating the wolf from *The Three Little Pigs*? Lots of oral-motor exercise! Gather several items that will easily move when they're blown on and a few that will not. Review with students the method the wolf used to try to destroy the pigs' houses. Then place an item on a table and invite a child (the wolf) to stand near it. Ask the remaining youngsters to predict whether the wolf will blow the object off the table; then prompt the wolf to huff and puff on the item to see whether the students' predictions come true. Ask students to explain why the wolf could or could not blow the item off the table. Then encourage exploration by asking, "What would happen if two wolves blew on the object?" After exploring the possibility, replace the item and choose a new wolf.

UNINVITED GUEST

Inspire interactive storytelling following a read-aloud of *Goldilocks and the Three Bears*. Place the suggested items in your dramatic-play area and encourage little ones to act out the story. Once youngsters are familiar with the tale, challenge them with a higher level of storytelling by changing the storyline. For example, Goldilocks becomes a little boy who enters a cottage containing items for a birthday celebration, such as three ice cream bowls, cupcakes, and gifts!

Suggested play items:
three appropriately sized stuffed
   toy bears
plastic bowls and spoons
chairs
boxes (beds)
a doll (Goldilocks)
cooking pot
mixing spoon

This One's Just Right!

After an oral reading of *Goldilocks and the Three Bears*, engage little ones in a fun art activity with a mathematical twist! Set out small, medium, and large bear cutouts (pattern on page 37; adjust size accordingly), paintbrushes that correspond to the sizes of the bears, paint, and craft items. Ask a child to select a bear and identify it as Papa Bear, Mama Bear, or Baby Bear, according to its size. Then ask, "What size paintbrush would be *just right* for painting [Baby Bear]?" Encourage her to compare the brush sizes to the size of her bear. After the youngster locates a corresponding brush, invite her to paint and decorate her bear.

Grab and Go

After a read-aloud of *Jack and the Beanstalk*, engage little ones in this game that focuses on beginning sounds. Attach a large paper beanstalk to the floor. Place at the top of the beanstalk several items that begin with /h/, such as a toy hen, horse, hammer, or horn; a hat; and a heart cutout. Invite a child (Jack) to crawl up the beanstalk. As he approaches the top, lead the remaining youngsters in chanting "Fee, fi, fo, fum! Hurry, Jack; you'd better run!" Prompt Jack to take an object and quickly climb down the beanstalk. Have Jack identify the item and its beginning sound. Repeat the process with other youngsters. After all the items have been collected, ask, "What is the same about each object's name?" Lead youngsters to notice that they all start with /h/. If desired, repeat the process with items that begin with a different sound.

Seed Search

Motivate your little seed searchers with this shake-and-match discovery center inspired by *Jack and the Beanstalk*! Obtain several varieties of dried beans. For each type of bean, partially fill a clear plastic jar with potting soil and then drop a few beans in the jar. Hot-glue a lid to each jar and shake it to conceal the beans. Put several of each type of bean in a separate resealable plastic bag and reinforce the seal with tape. A child chooses a jar and shakes it to reveal the hidden beans. Then he places the jar near the bag containing the same type of beans.

TEC61351

Farm

Down at the Farm

Rustle your little farmhands to your group area to act out imaginary farm chores. Lead youngsters in singing the song and performing the suggested action. Continue with additional verses, inserting words such as *feeds, digs, plants,* and *drives* accompanied by appropriate actions.

(sung to the tune of "The Muffin Man")

This is how the farmer [milks],
The farmer [milks], the farmer [milks],
This is how the farmer [milks]
Down on the farm each day!

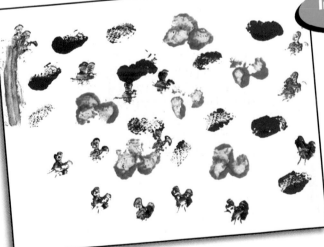

Farm Fresh

Inspire creative expression with playful produce art! Set out several produce items, such as a potato, a carrot, a stalk of celery, a pepper, and an apple (cut or uncut). Also provide shallow containers of paint, construction paper, a tub of water, and a veggie scrubber. A youngster dips an item in paint and presses, rolls, swipes, drags, or taps it on a sheet of paper. Then he uses the scrubber to clean the item in the tub of water. He continues with other produce, overlapping the prints and blending colors.

Independent play

Preschool Farm

Turn your dramatic-play area into a makeshift farm and watch imaginations and play skills soar!

Suggested play items: flannel shirts, rubber boots, straw hats, plastic produce, baskets, plastic eggs, cardboard box and brown crinkle shreds (chicken coop), stuffed toy farm animals, child-size tools (rake, shovel, and hoe), toy wheelbarrow, watering can, pails, rectangular planters (feeding and watering troughs), bale of straw, oversize cardboard box (tractor), large barn cutout attached to a wall

Teacher-guided play

Pass and Peep

Corral your clutch of chicks for a fun game that promotes listening and motor skills! Have students stand in a circle. Give a child a handled basket with several plastic eggs, most of them containing a large yellow pom-pom (chick). Play a recording of lively music and have youngsters pass the basket around the circle. Periodically stop the music and have the child with the basket open one of the eggs. If the egg contains a chick, little ones pretend to be baby chicks scratching their feet on the floor and saying "Peep, peep!" If the egg is empty, children stand quietly. Set that egg aside and restart the music.

Sheep Herders

Woof! Woof!

Gear up gross-motor muscles for this active outdoor game! Explain how farmers often use sheep dogs to herd, or move, their sheep or other livestock into a corral. Then designate a specific location as a sheep corral. Invite two or three youngsters to be sheep dogs and have the remaining youngsters (sheep) stand in an open area. On your signal, the sheep dogs chase the sheep, barking as they run. Each sheep that is tagged by a sheep dog goes to the corral. When all the sheep are in the corral, choose new sheep dogs and play another round!

Barnyard Banter

Encourage little ones to perform this little ditty farm animal–style! Lead youngsters in singing the song, prompting them to waddle and quack like ducks when the song ends. Continue in the same way, inserting other farm animal names and sounds where indicated and encouraging students to pretend to be the designated animal at the end of the song.

(sung to the tune of "The Farmer in the Dell")

A [duck] lives on the farm.
A [duck] lives on the farm.
"[Quack, quack]" is what it says.
A [duck] lives on the farm.

Continue with the following: *horse, neigh, neigh; hen, cluck, cluck; pig, oink, oink; cow, moo, moo; sheep, baa, baa; rooster, cock-a-doodle-doo*

Pig Play

Pigs love to play in mud and so will your little ones! Set out a plastic tub partially filled with potting soil mixed with a generous amount of water to make mud. Also provide plastic toy pigs and a container of clean water. A youngster manipulates the pigs in the mud, saying "Oink, oink!" as she plays. When she's finished, she gives each dirty piggy a bath!

In the Haystack

Intrigue youngsters with process art that becomes a peekaboo language activity! Provide large yellow haystack cutouts, a rolling pin wrapped with several rubber bands, and a shallow container of brown paint. A child rolls the rolling pin in the paint and then over the haystack. After the paint is dry, invite each child to cut out and glue a copy of the farm animal cards on page 43 to his haystack. Then help him glue a square cutout (flap) atop each card. To use the project, a child asks, "What is in the haystack?" Then he lifts a flap, identifies the animal, and mimics its sound.

Squirt!

Here's an "udderly" awesome way to build hand-eye coordination and hand strength! Fill several white, latex-free gloves with milk (or water tinted with white tempera paint). Tie the opening of each glove in a knot and poke a small hole in several of the fingers. Place the resulting udders in your water table along with a bucket. A youngster uses one hand to hold an udder above the bucket and the other hand to squeeze milk from the gloves' fingers into the bucket. He says "Moo! Moo!" as he simulates milking a cow.

Teacher-guided play

Sammy Scarecrow

Summon your tiny crows to the cornfield for some rhyme-time fun with Sammy Scarecrow! Hold up a decorative scarecrow (or pretend to be Sammy Scarecrow). Tell youngsters to listen carefully as Sammy announces two words (real or nonsense). Then have the group repeat the words and determine if they rhyme. If the words rhyme, have students (crows) pretend to fly around the room and back to the cornfield, saying "Caw! Caw!" as they fly. If the words do not rhyme, prompt the crows to stand still. Continue in the same way for several rounds or until interest wanes.

TEC61351

TEC61351

TEC61351

TEC61351

TEC61351

TEC61351

Feet

Independent play

Shoe Show

Promote interactive play skills when you invite little ones to manage a shoe store! Replace existing items in your dramatic-play area with the suggested items, and you're ready for business.

Suggested play items: assortment of adult and child-size footwear, shoeboxes for the footwear, customer chairs, foot measuring tool, employee nametags, toy cash register, play money, mock debit cards and checks, notepads (receipts), pencils or markers, telephone, footwear advertisements, business sign

---

Teacher-guided play

Tootsie Trail

Tiny tootsies get a sensory workout when they walk along this textured trail! To make a trail, attach to the floor a variety of textured materials, such as carpet squares, burlap, faux fur, corrugated cardboard, Bubble Wrap cushioning material, sandpaper, and rubber and straw doormats. Invite little ones to remove their shoes and stroll along the trail, encouraging them to comment on how the different textures feel. Guide them in using descriptive words related to the materials, such as *bumpy, scratchy, soft, furry,* and *rough.* Then ask questions such as the following: Which material felt the best when you stepped on it? Which material did you like stepping on least? Did any of the materials feel similar?

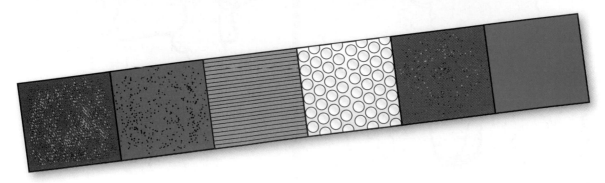

How Many Feet?

What has two feet? What has four feet? What has no feet? Invite youngsters to participate in this delightful ditty, and they'll find out! Lead little ones in singing the song, prompting them to mimic the specified animal at the end of each verse.

(sung to the tune of "The Farmer in the Dell")

A penguin has two feet.
A penguin has two feet.
Heigh-ho, just watch it go!
A penguin has two feet!　　　*Waddle like a penguin.*

A puppy has four feet.
A puppy has four feet.
Heigh-ho, just watch it go!
A puppy has four feet!　　　*Walk on hands and feet; bark like a puppy.*

An earthworm has no feet.
An earthworm has no feet.
Heigh-ho, just watch it go!
An earthworm has no feet!　　　*Wiggle on the floor like a worm.*

Continue with the following: *chicken, person (two feet); cow, kitten (four feet); snake (no feet)*

Sock Center

Matching skills multiply when you set up a mini laundromat for socks! Collect assorted pairs of socks in different sizes and styles. You may wish to include baby socks and booties, children's character socks, and adult-size socks. Also provide a makeshift washer and dryer, an empty laundry detergent box or bottle, a laundry basket, and a basket of spring-style clothespins. Youngsters pretend to wash and dry the socks. Then they find matching socks, clip them together, and put them in the laundry basket.

Footprints in the Dough

Develop visual discrimination and fine-motor skills when little ones make footprints. Set out play dough and small rolling pins. Also provide plastic toy figures with different numbers of feet in assorted shapes and sizes. For example, you might provide an elephant, a horse, a chicken, and a frog, along with child and adult people figures. Invite a child to flatten a lump of dough. Have her press the feet of desired figures in the dough; then encourage her to compare the sizes, shapes, and numbers of footprints. For an added challenge, have her close her eyes while you make footprints in the dough. Then ask her to open her eyes and guess the figures that made the footprints!

Left Foot, Right Foot

What kind of feet might a preschooler meet? Left and right, of course! To prepare for this fun game, attach a sticker to each child's right shoe, advising him that the shoe with the sticker is on his right foot and the shoe with no sticker is on his left foot. Then have youngsters practice which are their left feet and which are their right feet by pointing to them on command. After several practice rounds, call out simple directions—such as "Hop on your right foot," "Lift your left foot off the floor," and "Put your right foot forward"—for your youngsters to follow.

Mama Octopus

Entice youngsters with a silly group game! Conceal in a sack eight pieces of footwear (see suggestions) and several nonfootwear items. Attach eight crepe paper strips to a paper plate (Mama Octopus). Introduce Mama Octopus, and then guide students in counting her legs aloud. Next, tell little ones you need help finding footwear for each of Mama's eight legs. Invite a volunteer to take an item from the sack. Ask, "Can you wear a [item's name] on your foot?" If the answer is yes, have the student place the item near one of the octopus's legs. If the answer is no, have him tell where the item would be worn and then set it aside. Continue until Mama Octopus has all her footwear.

Suggested footwear items: sneaker, shoe, slipper, sock, sandal, flip-flop, snow boot, rain boot

Shoe Shopping

Visual memory skills get a workout with this shoe-themed game! Gather pairs of shoes and put one shoe from each pair in a separate shoebox. Place the remaining shoes on a nearby shelf. To begin, display each boxed shoe and then replace the lid. Next, invite a child to pretend she is shoe shopping. Have her browse the shoes on the shelf and choose one she wants to "buy." Then have her select the box she believes holds its match. Prompt her to remove the lid to see if the shoes match. If they do, have her put the shoe in the box and place it aside. If they do not, have her replace the shoebox lid and return the shoe to the shelf. Play continues until each shoebox contains a matching pair of shoes.

Five Senses

Teacher-guided play

The Nose Knows

Little ones will eagerly join in this sniff-and-match activity! Gather several small containers, such as margarine tubs, and poke a few holes in each lid. Place in each container a familiar item with a distinct aroma, such as an onion slice, chopped garlic, a pickle, and an orange slice. Display a duplicate set of items on separate paper plates. To begin, invite a child to sniff each of the exposed items. Then have her choose a container and sniff the scent through the lid. Ask her to place the container near the item she thinks gives off the same aroma; then encourage her to continue until each container is paired with an item. When she's finished, prompt her to remove each lid to see if the aromatic items match.

Independent play

Syrup Sacks

These easy-to-make sensory sacks are perfect for a soothing and entertaining tactile experience! Simply fill several resealable plastic bags with white corn syrup and add a few drops of food coloring to each bag. Seal each bag and reinforce the seal with packing tape. Set the bags at a table along with a few letter or number cards, if desired. Then invite youngsters to manipulate the bags and use their fingertips to draw or write on them for a soothing, multiskill-developing sensory experience.

Listen Up!

What happens when youngsters listen to sounds without seeing the objects that make them? They sharpen their auditory skills! Display several musical instruments, such as a drum, rhythm sticks, a triangle, and a bell. Help students identify each instrument and then have them listen to its sound. Next, instruct little ones to close their eyes and listen closely as you briefly play one of the instruments. Then, with their eyes still closed, ask them to guess what instrument you played. After each child has had the opportunity to guess, have youngsters open their eyes. Then reveal the instrument so students can see whether they were correct. Continue in the same way with the other instruments.

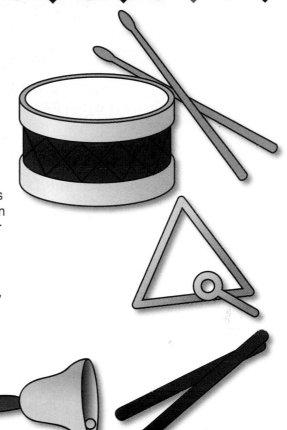

Pop! Pop! Pop!

Youngsters love the sensation and sound of Bubble Wrap cushioning material popping between their fingers, but what about using it under their feet? Try this idea for a fun gross-motor workout with a tactile twist! Attach large sheets of Bubble Wrap cushioning material to the floor and have youngsters remove their shoes. (Hint: Big bubbles work great for this activity!) Then play some lively music and invite little ones to show off their best dance moves atop the bubbly dance floor! Step one, two…pop!

Herbal Investigation

Here's a discovery activity that appeals to multiple senses! Display a variety of fresh herbs for children to touch, smell, taste, and examine with magnifying glasses. Guide youngsters in observing the color, texture, shape, size, and scent of the herbs. Ask sensory-related questions, such as the following: Which herb is your favorite to smell? Is there an herb that you think smells bad? What could you do with the herbs? Before each child ends his herbal investigation, invite him to glue herbs to a large leaf cutout. Then place the leaf in your discovery center.

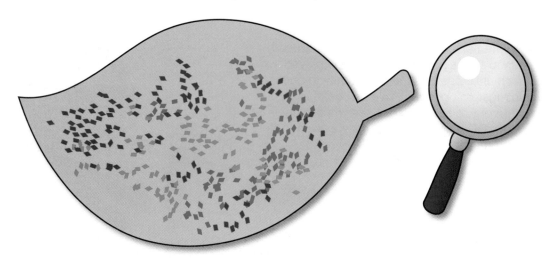

Blindfold Challenge

Put youngsters' tactile sense to the test! Glue tactile materials to a sheet of poster board. (Consider using cotton, sandpaper, Bubble Wrap cushioning material, crumpled aluminum foil, fabric fur, corrugated cardboard, ribbon, and a twig.) To begin, review with students each item on the poster board. Then invite a child to play and cover her eyes with a sleep mask. Have her touch the board, encouraging her to feel an item and tell what it is. After identifying the item, prompt her to remove the mask to see whether she is correct. Then repeat the process with other youngsters, changing the orientation of the board during play.

A Quick Peek

Increase visual awareness, focus, and language skills with this engaging, fast-paced activity! Tear from a magazine a page that shows a colorful picture or familiar scene. Place the page facedown in your lap, and then tell youngsters to watch carefully as you give them a quick peek at the picture. Display the page for just a moment, and then quickly put it facedown again. Ask, "What can you tell me about the picture?" After youngsters share what they saw, reveal the picture again for a slightly longer time and have students share again. After repeating the process several times, display the page for youngsters to examine and describe.

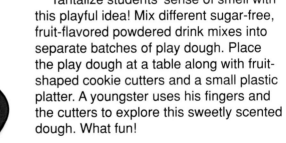

Fruit Platter

Tantalize students' sense of smell with this playful idea! Mix different sugar-free, fruit-flavored powdered drink mixes into separate batches of play dough. Place the play dough at a table along with fruit-shaped cookie cutters and a small plastic platter. A youngster uses his fingers and the cutters to explore this sweetly scented dough. What fun!

Gardening

Vegetable Soup

Is it a fruit or a vegetable? After visiting this mock produce stand, youngsters will readily know the answers! Display real or plastic fruits and vegetables near your group area. Place in the area a soup pot and a ladle. Say to youngsters, "I'd like to make a pot of soup and could use help picking out the vegetables. Who would like to help?" Hand a volunteer a toy shopping basket and ask him to go to the produce stand and "buy" a vegetable for the soup. When he returns, have him identify the chosen item. If the group agrees it is a garden veggie, have the child put it in the pot and stir the soup. If not, thank him for his help and set the item aside. Continue with other volunteers until all the veggies are in the pot. Then give each child an imaginary bowl of soup to sip!

Independent play

Perfect Potatoes

Pique curiosity and increase attention to detail when your tiny harvesters dig into this discovery center! Fill your sensory table with potting soil and bury real potatoes under the soil. Provide plastic shovels, a pail, magnifying glasses, a cloth tape measure, and a balance scale. Encourage students to unearth the potatoes and use the tools to investigate, measure, and weigh the harvested produce.

Gorgeous Garden

Foster pretend and collaborative play when you turn your block area into an indoor flower garden! Add the suggested props to the area and use the blocks to create planters, edging, and walls!

Suggested play items: green outdoor carpet or bulletin board paper (garden), plastic gardening tools, child-size wheelbarrow, watering can, foam kneeling pads, gardening gloves, aprons, sun hats, plastic planters, empty seed packets, garden markers, silk flowers, floral foam (flower arranging), plastic garden fence, plastic garden decor

Tiny Seeds

Gather your little gardeners for some imaginary planting. Lead them in performing the song shown, guiding them to understand that seeds need soil, water, and sunlight to grow.

(sung to the tune of "The Itsy-Bitsy Spider")

I dug into the soil	*Squat down; pretend to dig the dirt.*
And planted tiny seeds.	*Pretend to plant seed.*
I patted down the dirt	*Pat the floor with hand.*
And threw away the weeds.	*Pretend to toss away weeds.*
Next, came the rain	*Wiggle fingers as if raining.*
And the sun with all its power.	*Make a large circle with arms.*
Then the itsy-bitsy seeds	*Slowly stand.*
Grew into pretty flowers!	*Stretch arms up and out.*

In the Garden

Introduce little ones to an array of fascinating bugs with a rhythmic read-aloud of *Over in the Garden* by Jennifer Ward. In advance, copy and cut out a class supply of bug cards from page 55 and scatter them around the room (garden). After the read-aloud, have each child find one card and return to her seat. Review each two-page spread in the book, encouraging students with a corresponding card to hold it in the air. Guide the group in identifying and counting aloud the bugs; then prompt each youngster with that card to pretend to be the critter.

Super Soil

This process art fosters imaginative thinking and develops fine-motor skills! Set out green construction paper and a small plastic bucket filled with a mixture of brown paint and sand (soil). Provide a plastic hand shovel along with brown, black, and white paper scraps. A child uses the shovel to scoop soil and then, on a sheet of paper, drags the soil so it resembles the dirt in a garden. He repeats the process until a desired effect is achieved. Then he tears "seeds" from the paper scraps and "plants" them in the soil.

TEC61351

TEC61351

TEC61351

TEC61351

TEC61351

TEC61351

TEC61351

TEC61351

TEC61351

TEC61351

Healthy Me

B-R-U-S-H!

Motivate youngsters to practice good oral hygiene with the help of this catchy tune! Lead little ones in performing the suggested actions as a reminder to brush their teeth twice a day.

(sung to the tune of "Bingo")

My dentist told me, "Brush your teeth.   *Point finger as if advising.*
Please, brush them twice a day, now."   *Hold up two fingers.*
B-R-U-S-H!   *Pretend to brush with finger.*
B-R-U-S-H!
B-R-U-S-H!
"Please, brush them twice a day, now."   *Hold up two fingers.*

Independent play **Splish, Splash!**

Little ones will actually look forward to bath time with this pretend play idea! Provide the suggested props, and youngsters will be eager to take an imaginary bath.

Suggested play items: large cardboard box (bathtub); bath mat; bath towels; washcloths or bath sponge; empty bottles of shampoo, conditioner, bubble bath, and body wash; block (soap); rubber ducks; child-size bathrobe; slippers

Ah-choo!

Boost health and hygiene skills when little ones learn to properly cover a sneeze! Have students sit in a circle. Place a small trash can in the center of the circle and hand a child a box of tissues. Have youngsters pass the tissues around the circle as you lead them in singing the song shown. At the end of the song, direct the child holding the box to take a tissue, cover his nose with it, and say, "Ah-choo!" Have him toss the tissue in the trash can and pretend to wash his hands. Continue in the same way until each child has had a turn or until interest wanes. As an alternative, teach little ones to sneeze into their arm for times when a tissue is not available.

(sung to the tune of "The Farmer in the Dell")

I have an itchy nose.
I need the tissues, please.
I think I might need one
Because I just might sneeze!

Teacher-guided play

Pea Soup, Please!

Looking for a fun way to teach little ones about healthy eating? Try pea soup! Set out a soup pot, a large spoon, and a bowl of green pom-poms (peas). Ask youngsters to think about foods that are healthy to eat. Then invite a volunteer to name a healthy food, with help as needed, and have her take a pea from the bowl and toss it into the pot. Continue until each student has had a turn. Then stir the soup and let each child pretend to take a taste.

Muddy Hands

Invite your little ones to get messy in a center that leads to good hygiene! Prepare a tray with brown fingerpaint thickened with flour (mud). Place near the sink a bottle of liquid hand soap and a supply of white paper towels. Invite a youngster to play in the mud, encouraging her to squish and spread the mud as well as draw or write in it with her fingers. When she's finished playing in the mud, guide her in properly washing and drying her hands.

Pearly Whites

Brush, brush, brush! This fun activity promotes dental health care! Set out a laminated cutout copy of page 59 (or slide the cutout into a page protector). Provide dry-erase markers, a small tube of toothpaste, a toothbrush, and a container of baby wipes. A child draws marks on the teeth, pretending the teeth are unclean from eating. Then he gently squeezes a small amount of toothpaste on the toothbrush and brushes the teeth. When he's finished brushing, he wipes the mouth with a baby wipe. Then he checks to see whether there are any food particles left on the teeth.

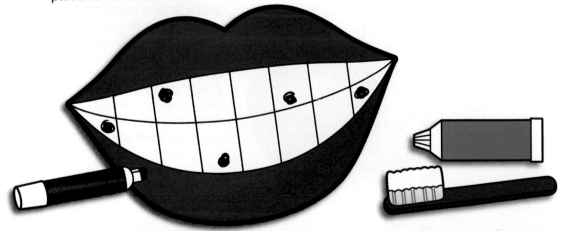

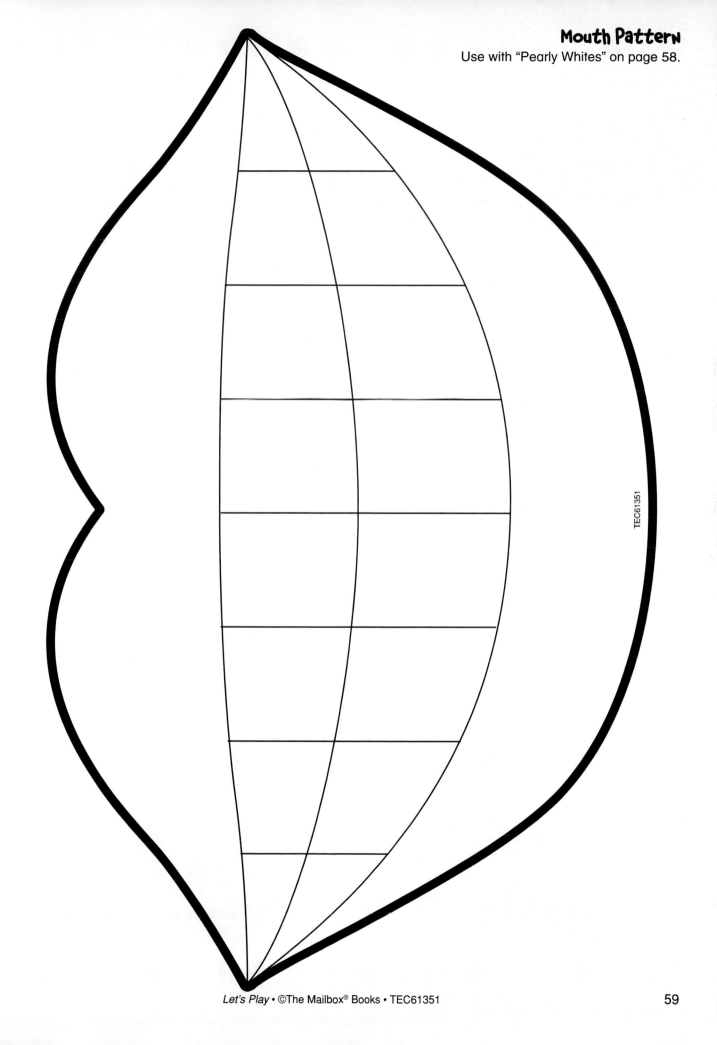

TEC61351

Home

Home Is Where the Heart Is

Are all homes the same size, shape, and style? Youngsters discover that there are many different types of homes with this real estate review! Post magazine pictures of different homes. Then invite youngsters to board an imaginary bus and take them on a home tour. Stop at each home to briefly discuss it. When the tour ends, gather the pictures and guide youngsters in discussing the similarities and differences in the homes. Ask questions such as "Do you think you would see a farmhouse and an igloo in the same neighborhood?" and "Would you rather live in a castle or a log cabin?"

Model Homes

Develop planning skills and encourage collaboration when you put youngsters in charge of home construction! Simply add the suggested materials to your existing building blocks.

Suggested play items: real estate magazines, discarded blueprints or blue paper and white crayons, toy construction tools, hard hats, safety goggles, safety cones, plastic interlocking blocks, empty oatmeal and potato chip canisters (pillars), cardboard tubes, PVC pipe pieces

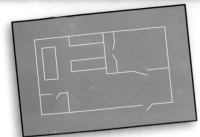

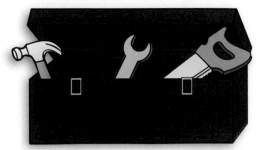

Teacher-guided play

Favorite Spaces

Build expressive language skills when you invite little ones to share about their homes. Have students sit in a circle and hand one child a house cutout. Lead youngsters in singing the song as they pass the cutout around the circle. When the song ends, encourage the child holding the cutout to tell which room in his home is his favorite and why. Continue the game until each child has had the opportunity to share.

(sung to the tune of "The Muffin Man")

Oh, do you have a favorite room,
A favorite room, a favorite room?
Oh, do you have a favorite room?
Please tell us what it is!

Independent play

Beach-Front Property

Inspire young imaginations to think beyond sand castles when you designate your sand table as beach-front property! Provide plastic interlocking blocks, plastic trees, medium-size shells, outdoor dollhouse furniture, and people figures. Encourage little ones to build vacation homes along the beach and then dive into creative play.

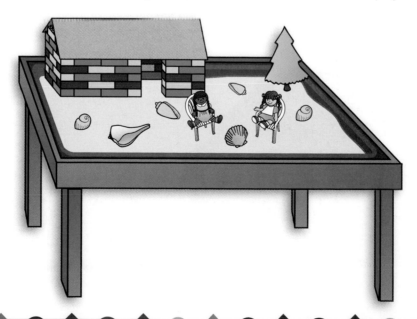

What Am I?

Engage critical-thinking skills when you challenge youngsters to a guessing game that features household clues! To play, think of an object you might find in a home, such as a refrigerator, sofa, bed, or bathtub. Then provide clues to help little ones guess the object. When the correct item is guessed, ask, "Where in a home would you find a [object name]?" Encourage students to tell the object's typical location. For added fun, periodically give clues for something not typically found inside a home, such as a cow or a swimming pool. Then ask the same follow-up question, which is sure to elicit lots of giggles and responses!

Independent play

Happy Habitats

Turn your water table into a sea habitat! Float an assortment of plastic or craft foam sea and land animals in the water. Place a large tray (land) near the table and provide a handheld fishnet or a slotted spoon. A child scoops an animal out of the water and then decides whether the animal's home is in water or on land. If the animal lives in water, he tosses it back in. If the animal lives on land, he sets it on the tray. He continues until all the animals are in the appropriate habitats.

Dishwasher Fun

Boost self-esteem, independence, and responsibility with some playtime table-setting. Provide placemats, napkins, and play food. Then place plastic dinnerware in a box (dishwasher). Youngsters "unload" the dishwasher and set a table for a meal. Then they serve themselves food, pretend to eat a delicious meal, and "load" their dirty dinnerware back into the dishwasher.

Cheer for Chores!

What happens when more than one person pitches in to help with household chores? Youngsters will learn the answer firsthand! You will need a watch or a clock with a second hand. Dump a container of toys onto the floor and ask, "What will happen if no one cleans up these toys?" After little ones share their thoughts, invite a volunteer to put the toys back in the container as you time her. Repeat the activity two more times, adding an additional volunteer each time. Be sure to encourage the rest of the group to cheer their classmates on! After all three challenges are complete, help youngsters compare the cleanup times, leading them to understand that working together helps get chores done faster and easier.

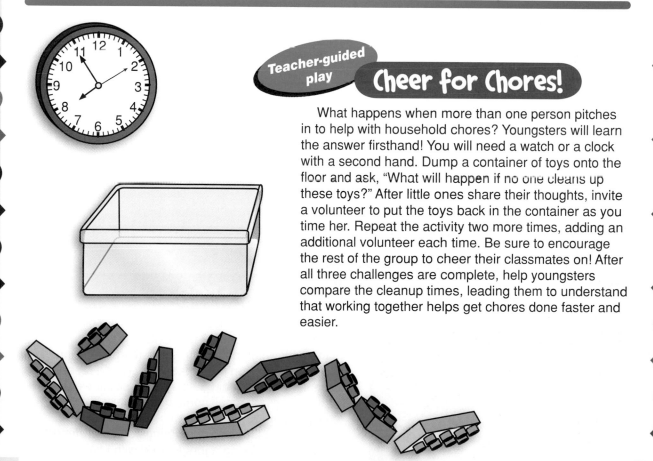

Jungle

Teacher-guided play
Run Away!

What would it be like to walk through a jungle? Would it be peaceful, scary, or exciting? Ask youngsters to imagine they're on a jungle safari. Invite them to tell what they see and how it makes them feel. Then lead little ones in singing this fun action song!

(sung to the tune of "Ring Around the Rosie")

Walking through the jungle,	Walk in place.
The ground starts to rumble.	
Tigers! Tigers!	Stomp your feet.
Run far away!	Run in place.
Running past the trees,	Run in place.
And what should my eyes see?	
Monkeys! Monkeys!	Pretend to be a monkey.
Run far away!	Run in place.
Climbing up a vine,	Pretend to climb.
I thought that things were fine.	
Snakes! Snakes!	Maneuver arms like a snake.
Run far away!	Run in place.
I'm walking near a river.	Walk in place.
My body starts to quiver.	
Crocodiles! Crocodiles!	Motion hands like crocodile mouth.
Run far away!	Run in place.

Independent play
Frog Fun

Little ones will hop right into creative play when you turn your sensory table into a jazzy jungle! Fill the table with potting soil, trees (cardboard tubes with construction paper leaves or green crepe paper strips), medium-size rocks, silk flowers, twigs (logs), a small container partially filled with water (pond), and an assortment of colorful plastic frogs. Encourage youngsters to pretend they are exploring a jungle filled with exotic frogs.

Jungle Explorers

Ignite a sense of curiosity and adventure when you invite youngsters to explore your classroom jungle! Decorate the classroom with real or artificial plants and flowers to create a jungle-like atmosphere. Place plastic or stuffed toy jungle animals around the room. Also provide toy binoculars (or ones made from cardboard tubes), a safari hat, and a clipboard and writing tool. A youngster walks through the jungle and draws a check mark for each animal he observes. When he's finished exploring, he counts the marks to determine the total number of animals.

Fantastic Foliage

Sharpen cutting skills when you invite little ones to create jungle foliage. Draw oversize leaf shapes on large green construction paper. Set out colorful tissue paper scraps, glue, and scissors. Also provide a nonfiction book or magazine with photos of jungle foliage. Invite students to browse the photos for inspiration, prompting them to describe interesting or unusual foliage. Encourage youngsters to cut out the construction paper leaves and glue on tissue paper flowers. Then help students mount the foliage around the room with brown or green crepe paper vines to simulate a jungle habitat!

Monkey Business

This jungle-themed rhyme beckons youngsters to monkey around! Invite five students to mimic monkeys as you lead their classmates in reciting the first verse of the rhyme. At the end of the third line, prompt one of the monkeys to "run away." Repeat the verse until there is one monkey left in the tree. Then recite the second verse to conclude the rhyme.

[Five] little monkeys playing in a tree,
One looked down and spotted me.
It got scared and ran away.
[Four] little monkeys stayed to play.

One little monkey playing in the tree,
It looked down and spotted me.
It got scared and ran away.
No little monkeys stayed to play!

Safari Scavenger Hunt

Send youngsters on a safari scavenger hunt! Cut out a class supply of cards from page 67 and scatter them around the room. Ask each child to find one card and bring it to your group area. Invite a student to hold her card in the air and identify the animal. Then encourage each youngster who has a matching card to hold it in the air. Invite each child displaying a card to mimic the animal. Then help the children arrange the cards in the same row of a pocket chart. Repeat the process for each card. Then lead youngsters in counting the animals in each row and comparing the rows.

TEC61351

TEC61351

TEC61351

TEC61351

TEC61351

TEC61351

Nursery Rhymes

Teacher-guided play

Oh No, Spider Bowl!

Here's a fun, not-so-scary spider game! Gather two or three disposable bowls and draw a spider on the bottom of one. Have youngsters sit in a circle and hand each bowl to a different child. Tell little ones there are no sneak peeks at the bottom of the bowls! To play, have youngsters pass the bowls around the circle as you lead the group in reciting "Little Miss Muffet." At the end of the rhyme, direct each child with a bowl to turn it over. Prompt the child with the spider bowl to say, "Oh no, spider bowl!" and drop the bowl and "run" away. Have her return to her seat, and continue play for several more rounds.

Independent play

Wonderful Walls

How many times can youngsters recite the "Humpty Dumpty" rhyme? Countless times—when they transform your block area into a wonderland of walls! Simply add the suggested items to your block collection along with a copy of "Humpty Dumpty." Encourage little ones to build a variety of walls and then reenact the rhyme!

Suggested play items: cardboard blocks, foam blocks, plastic interlocking blocks, bristle blocks, cardboard boxes, plastic eggs decorated to resemble Humpty Dumpty, sanitized egg cartons (for walls and storing eggs)

The Clock Strikes...

The clock struck one in "Hickory Dickory Dock," but why not explore other times of day as well! Give each child a rhythm instrument and display a toy clock with moveable hands. Set the clock to one o'clock, pointing out the time and the position of the hands to youngsters. Then lead students in reciting "Hickory Dickory Dock," pausing at the end of the third line and prompting each child to play his instrument the appropriate number of times to represent the designated hour. Reposition the clock hands and repeat the process, inserting the matching hour in the rhyme each time.

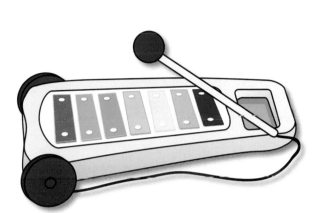

Mischievous Mouse

Highlight positional words with a little mouse mischief! Attach a paper plate clockface to one end of a rectangular box to make a grandfather clock. Glue a length of yarn to a large gray pom-pom to make a mouse. Recite the altered nursery rhyme shown, skittering the mouse around the clock as you say the words. At the end of the last line, position the mouse *on top of, beside, in front of, behind,* or *above* the clock and prompt youngsters to identify the mouse's position. For added fun, position the mouse somewhere on or near a student!

Hickory dickory dock,
The mouse ran up the clock.
The clock struck one;
The mouse ran down;
Now, where can the mouse be found?

Get Well, Jack and Jill!

After reciting the rhyme "Jack and Jill," elicit feelings of empathy and thoughtfulness by encouraging youngsters to make get-well cards! Ask little ones if they have ever taken a tumble and gotten hurt. Then ask, "How do you think Jack and Jill felt when they tumbled down that big hill?" After a brief discussion, invite little ones to make get-well cards using pail cutouts and craft materials, such as stickers, watercolors, and crayons or markers. Encourage each child to dictate a message to Jack and Jill for you to write on his card. If desired, display the cards with a large well cutout and the title "Jack and Jill Took Quite a Spill!"

Jack and Jill,
I hope you feel better!
Love, Caleb

Fetching Water

Inspire your little Jacks and Jills to explore capacity in this playful center! Place a large plastic tub (well) in your water table and fill it with water. Float a pail in the water. Place assorted containers around the well. A student dips the pail in the well and then pours the water into a container. As the child plays, encourage her to explore capacity by asking questions such as "Do you think you will need a full pail of water to fill the small green container?"

Lost and Found

Little Bo Peep has lost her sheep and needs a team to find them! Hide a class supply of sheep cutouts (see pattern below) around the room where they can easily be found. After leading youngsters in reciting the rhyme, pretend to be Bo Peep and say in your saddest Bo Peep voice, "Please help me find my lost sheep!" Have an adult helper assist the students in gathering all the sheep. While students search, keep your back to the group and repeat in a sad voice, "Oh dear, I think my sheep are lost forever!" After all the children have found a sheep, the helper prompts the group to surprise you by saying, "Don't cry, Bo Peep! We found your sheep!" Then collect your sheep with great fanfare, giving each little sheepherder a hug or high-five!

Sheep Pattern
Use with "Lost and Found" above.

TEC61351

Ocean

What Lives There?

Invite little ones on an imaginary adventure to find out what they know about ocean critters! Ask youngsters to pretend they are deep-sea diving. As they "swim" around, encourage them to name creatures they might see and describe what the creatures look like and how they move. Next, lead little ones in singing several verses of the song below, substituting the name of a different ocean creature each time and encouraging little ones to move like that creature.

(sung to the tune of "My Bonnie Lies Over the Ocean")

I wish that I lived in the ocean.
Yes, that is the best place for me!
And if I did live in the ocean,
[A sea star] is what I would be!

[Sea star, sea star],
[A sea star] is what I would be, would be.
[Sea star, sea star],
[A sea star] is what I would be!

Continue with the following: *octopus, sea turtle, lobster, shark, crab, jellyfish, sea horse, whale*

Scootin' Sharks

Youngsters develop gross-motor skills as they investigate that fascinating ocean animal, the shark! Scatter fish cutouts on the floor and provide scooter boards. Little ones scoot around on their bellies pretending to be sharks. When they are hungry, they pick up fish and pretend to eat them. What fun!

Water and Waves

Youngsters make ocean wave masterpieces with this idea! Provide a variety of different brushes. Then encourage each child to investigate the brushes as he uses them to cover a sheet of paper with blue and green paint. While the paint is still wet, prompt him to dip a length of yarn into white paint and then drag it repeatedly across the project. The resulting lines will look like whitecaps on ocean waves!

Play Dough Creatures

Here's a center that encourages little ones to investigate living things through play! Trim a length of blue bulletin board paper as shown. If desired, add ocean details to the paper. Then laminate it for durability. Place the paper at a table along with play dough. Little ones visit the table and manipulate the dough to make ocean creatures. Then they engage in imaginary play with their creations!

Shells and Shovels

Little ones can sort seashells and explore their textures with this sand table activity! Bury seashells in your sand table and then moisten the sand to give it an authentic beach texture. Stock the table with plastic sand pails and shovels. Youngsters search for the seashells and place them in the buckets, exploring their texture and sorting them as desired. They can even create sand castles with the moist sand and add the shells as decorations!

The Jellyfish Jive

Youngsters have their very own tentacles for this jellyfish dance. Give each youngster crepe paper streamers (tentacles). Then play a recording of slow music and encourage little ones to "float" about the room, wiggling their tentacles as they go. Next, play a recording of fast music, prompting your little jellyfish to move accordingly.

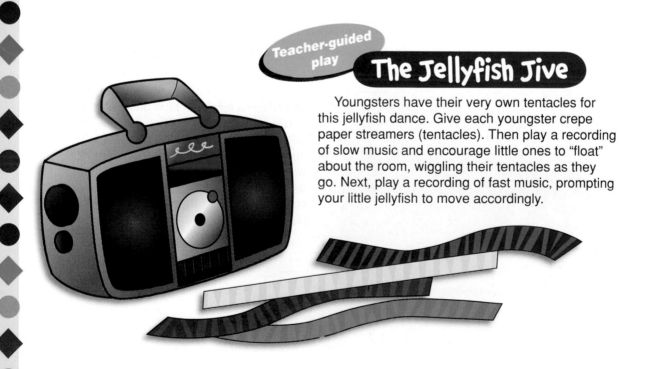

Let's Surf!

What fabulous individual sport is played in the ocean? Why, surfing of course! Cut surf board shapes from cardboard or poster board and place them in an open area. Show youngsters photos or videos of people surfing. Then encourage little ones to visit the area and pretend to surf! If desired, play a recording of beach music to add atmosphere to this cute center!

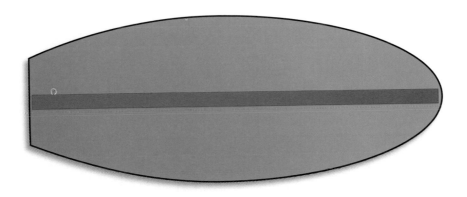

Fish Count

Encourage little ones to dive for fish! Scatter fish cutouts on your floor and then give a youngster a net. Say, "My goodness, I am so hungry I could eat five fish from the ocean!" Prompt the child to pretend to dive and swim, catching five fast-moving fish! When he brings them back, pretend to gobble them up. Then repeat the activity with a different volunteer and number of fish. When all the fish have been eaten, scatter them on the floor again.

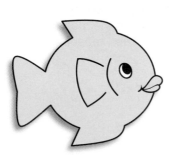

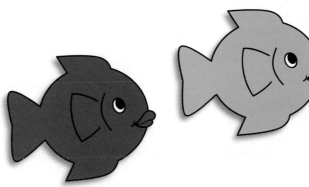

Outer Space

Teacher-guided play

Starstruck

What happens when little ones create personalized representations of a starry night? They fine-tune their pincer grasps and engage in wishful thinking! Set out black construction paper, white circle cutouts (moons), and foil star stickers. Invite each child to glue a moon to a sheet of paper. Then have her peel stars from their backings and press them on the paper to create a starry sky. As students work, guide them in reciting the rhyme "Star Light, Star Bright." Then encourage each child to close her eyes and make a wish for you to record on her project.

I wish I had a new puppy!

Teacher-guided play

10, 9, 8...Blastoff!

Invite your little astronauts to the launchpad for an imaginary trip into outer space! Lead youngsters in performing the song shown. At the end of the song, have students pretend to buckle themselves into a spacecraft. After everyone is safely buckled in, lead little ones in counting backward from ten to zero, prompting them to shout "Blast off!" at the appropriate time to begin their journey into outer space. After a few moments, pretend to land on the moon or a planet and invite youngsters to describe what they "see." Then repeat the countdown and blastoff for the return trip.

(sung to the tune of "If You're Happy and You Know It")

Ten, nine, eight, seven, six, Five, Four, three, two, one, zero...blastoff!

Let's get ready for our trip to outer space!
Let's get ready for our trip to outer space!
What a fascinating place—
Way up there in outer space.
Let's get ready for our trip to outer space!

Moonscape

Creative play is sure to skyrocket when you turn your sand table into a miniature moonscape! Generously dampen the sand and provide space-related toys and balls of aluminum foil (moon rocks). Also provide circular objects, such as a film canister, a cork, and a small plastic jar. Youngsters use the circular objects to make holes (craters) in the sand. Then they use the other props to engage in pretend outer space play.

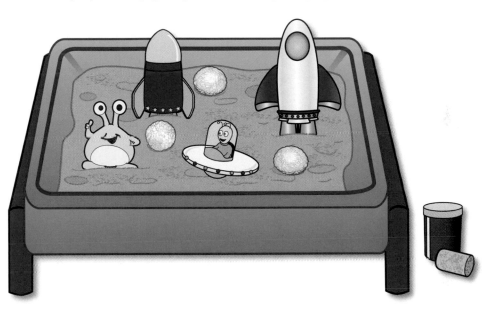

Space Adventures

Create an atmosphere that ignites imagination and watch as pretend play skills blast off! Simply attach star stickers and planet cutouts to a length of bulletin board paper and display the resulting mural in your center. Then provide the suggested items.

Suggested play items: large appliance box with door and makeshift control panel (spacecraft), football or bicycle helmets, boots, gloves, walkie-talkies, play food in storage bags, stuffed backpacks (oxygen tanks), clipboards and writing tools (for recording space adventures), rocks (moon rocks)

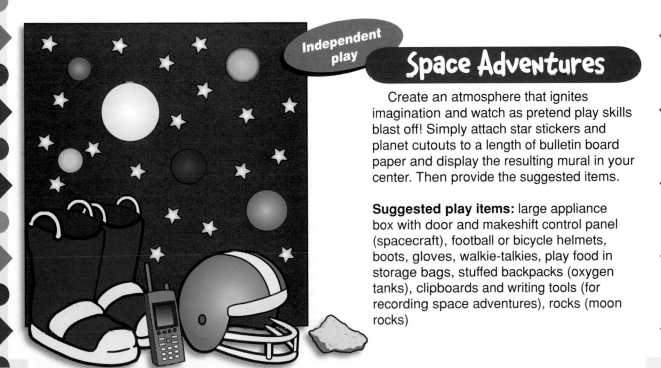

Sensitive Sun

Mr. Sun makes learning the /s/ sound fun! Cut out a yellow copy of the sun rays on page 79. Set out a yellow circle (Mr. Sun) and a tagboard smile. (If desired, place sunglasses on the sun.) Display a ray and have youngsters say the picture word. If the word begins with /s/, place the smile on Mr. Sun and say, "This word makes Mr. Sun smile!" Then invite a child to place the ray near the sun. If the word begins with a different sound, display the smile upside-down and say, "Uh-oh, this word makes Mr. Sun frown!" and set the ray aside. Repeat the process with each remaining ray. Then review the picture names on the rays by Mr. Sun.

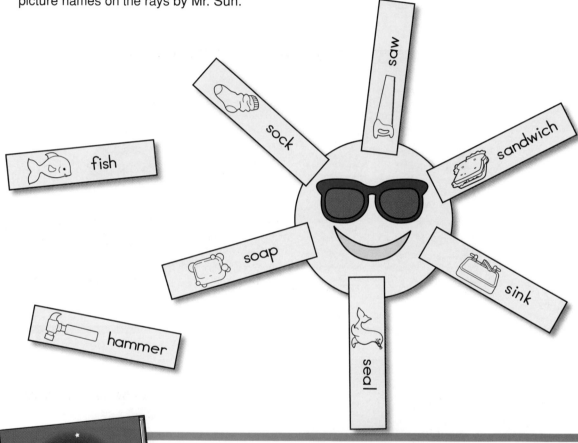

saw

sock

sandwich

fish

soap

sink

hammer

seal

Outer Space

Crater Creations

Little ones' finger muscles and imaginations get a workout with this fun idea! Set out white play dough, corks, blunt toothpicks, and a book or magazine that shows details of the moon's surface. Also provide small space-related toys and figures. A child shapes the play dough into a ball. Then, using the provided tools, he continues to mold the play dough so it resembles the moon's surface. When he's finished, he engages in pretend play using the space toys.

soap

TEC61351

sock

TEC61351

saw

TEC61351

sandwich

TEC61351

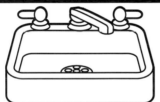

sink

TEC61351

seal

TEC61351

fish

TEC61351

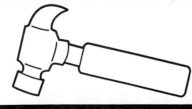

hammer

TEC61351

Pets

Teacher-guided play
Simple Needs

Reinforce the basic needs of pets with this toe-tapping ditty. Lead youngsters in singing the song shown. Then continue with each suggested verse.

(sung to the tune of "The Farmer in the Dell")

A pet needs [food to eat].
A pet needs [food to eat].
Pets have needs just like us.
A pet needs [food to eat].

Continue with the following: *fresh water, a safe home, exercise, lots of love*

Teacher-guided play
A Perfect Pet

Which pet should I get? This is the question the little girl ponders throughout *I Want a Pet* by Lauren Child. Read the story aloud. Then ask a youngster what she thinks is inside the egg at the end of the story. Have little ones move and make noises like the pet she suggests. Then ask another student to share his thoughts. Continue with each remaining youngster.

Caring for Pets

Encourage your little veterinarians to care for a variety of patients. Place the suggested items in your dramatic-play area to transform it into a veterinarian's office.

Suggested play items: stuffed toy animals (patients), thermometer, cloth bandages, rolls of gauze, cotton balls, toy syringe, leash, toy pet carrier, food and water bowls, dog treats, brush, large white button-up shirts (doctor's coats), clipboards, paper, crayons

Teacher-guided play

A Hungry Pup

Practice number skills with this engaging small-group game! Label each of several bone cutouts with a desired number. Give each child a bone and then slip on a dog puppet. Tell the group that this dog is very hungry and loves to eat bones. Make the dog bark a desired number of times as the youngsters count its barks. Then direct the child holding the bone with the matching number to "feed" the bone to the dog. Continue until the dog has eaten all the bones!

Bark, bark, bark!

3

Pet Tales

Independent play

Encourage your preschoolers to read their favorite books about pets to an eager group of listeners. In your reading area, set out a selection of books about pets along with stuffed toy pets. A child chooses a couple of pets and a book. Then she finds a cozy spot and "reads" the book to the pets. If your class has a class pet, invite a student to take a book to the class pet's home and "read" the book to the pet.

Trainer Says

Independent play

Trainer says roll over!

Little ones become well-trained pups in this version of Simon Says! Explain to youngsters that they are going to pretend to be puppies learning new tricks and you will pretend to be the trainer. Give commands such as "Trainer says sit" or "Trainer says lay down," encouraging the pups to follow the commands.

Best in Show

Turn your classroom into an arena for this one-of-a-kind pet show. Prior to the beginning of the show, have each child tell you which type of pet he would like to pretend to be. Have youngsters sit in a large circle. To begin the show, announce a child's name and his chosen pet. Invite the child to walk around the circle pretending to be that type of pet. Prompt him to perform a trick. Continue until each child has had a turn. To conclude the show, award each child a ribbon cutout!

Favorite Pets

Find out your students' pets of choice with this amusing data-collection activity. Designate a sound (or movement) for each pet you wish to include in the activity. Then invite each child to make the sound of the pet of her choice. Students making the same sound find each other and stand together. After the groups are formed, compare them using words such as *more*, *fewer*, and *equal*.

Woof!

Squeak!

Meow!

Transportation

Teacher-guided play

Airplane Sing-Along

Summon little ones to your group area to take an imaginary flight aboard a jumbo jet! Simply lead youngsters in performing this engaging song.

(sung to the tune of "Take Me Out to the Ballgame")

Take me out to the airport.
I'll walk up to the gate.
I'll show my ticket and wave goodbye.
Now I can soar through the big open sky.
Watch me zoom, zoom, zoom! Look, I'm soaring
Above cars and buses and trains,
For it's great to fly through the sky
On a great big plane!

March in place.
March in place.
Show pretend ticket; wave goodbye.
Pretend to fly.

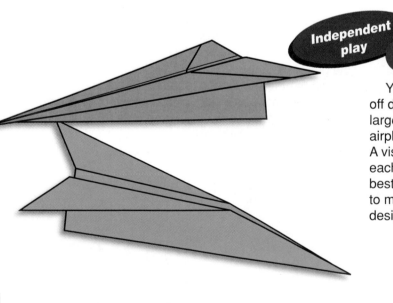

Independent play

Take Flight

Youngsters' exploration skills take off during this engaging activity. In a large open area, set out several paper airplanes along with blank paper. A visitor to the area gently throws each airplane, noting which ones fly best. Then he folds a sheet of paper to make a paper airplane of his own design to fly.

Teacher-guided play — Making Tracks

Set up this discovery center in your art area. Cover a tabletop with bulletin board paper. Provide shallow containers of paint and place a toy vehicle next to each container. Invite each child to choose a vehicle, dip its wheels in the paint, and then roll it across the paper. Then have him make a second set of tracks using another vehicle. Invite each youngster to repeat the steps several times. As students play, guide them in making observations about the colors and textures. Encourage exploration through thought-provoking questions such as "How did Peter make such a dark track?" and "I wonder what will happen when Nia makes a red track over that freshly painted blue track?"

Independent play — Sparkling Clean Cars

What happens when you turn your water table into a sudsy car wash? You give youngsters' fine-motor skills a tune-up! Whip several drops of liquid dish soap in the water; then provide a variety of scrubbers, towels for drying, and washable toy vehicles. To assess sorting and color identification skills, temporarily open the car wash to only a specific type or color of vehicle.

Transportation Riddles

Teacher-guided play

These entertaining riddles help students review different forms of transportation. Have students stand in a large open area. Read one of the riddles shown. Then invite youngsters to answer the riddle by moving around like that form of transportation.

I can fly in snow or rain.
I'm very fast. I am a ____. *(plane)*

I get wet. I can float.
I move in the water. I am a _. *(boat)*

I have four wheels. I can ride through the mud and muck.
I can carry stuff, because I am a _. *(truck)*

I don't use gas, but I like to eat hay.
I live in a barn, and I like to neigh. I'm a _. *(horse)*

I have two wheels and a seat for one.
You have to pedal me, which is so much fun. I am a _. *(bicycle)*

Cruising Along

Teacher-guided play

Preschoolers understand the importance of keeping their eyes on the road while driving! Attach tape to the floor so it resembles roads. Add a few obstacles—such as small traffic cones, a stop sign, and stuffed toy pedestrians—to the roads. Invite each child to pretend to get into her car, hold a paper plate steering wheel, and maneuver her car along the roads as she steers clear of the obstacles.

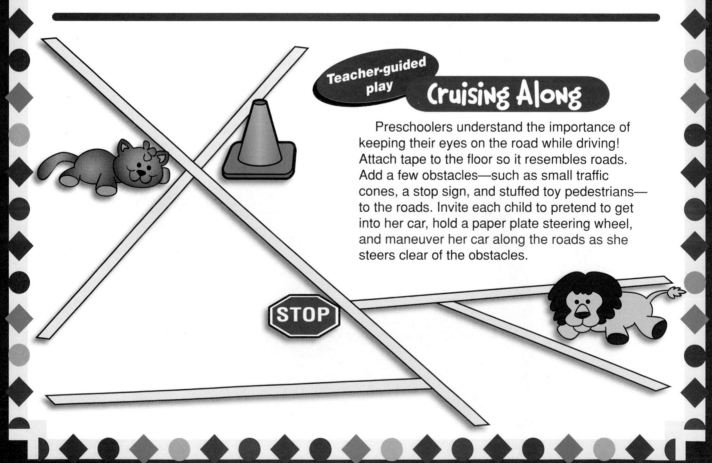

Teacher-guided play

Tickets, Please

All aboard for color-recognition practice! Use several colors of construction paper to cut out a class supply of train tickets. Then line up student chairs to create an imaginary train. Give each child a ticket and have them sit near the train. Put on a conductor's hat and stand near the back of the train. Announce a color. A child with a ticket of that color hands the ticket to you and then "boards" the train. After all the passengers are on the train, pretend to drive the train to a desired location. This versatile idea can easily be adapted to review other skills, such as letter, number, and shape recognition and counting.

Independent play

Sail Away

Encourage little ones to experiment with designing and building boats. Gather a supply of boat-building items, such as clean margarine or cream-cheese tubs, plastic lids, foam blocks, unused foam trays, clean milk cartons, sterilized egg cartons, play dough, straw, and paper scraps. Place the items near a large tub of water. A child uses the materials to build a boat of his own design. Then he puts his boat in the water.

Weather

Rainy Day Troubles

An unexpected downpour on a Saturday morning causes the townspeople to become cantankerous in *The Rain Came Down* by David Shannon. After reading the story aloud, make rain sounds by playing maracas or tapping a desk. During this rainstorm, prompt students to look grumpy and stomp around your large-group area. Then stop the rain and hold up a sun cutout, encouraging students to walk around smiling and shaking each others' hands. Continue for several rounds.

A Wacky Rainbow

Brighten up your classroom with these unique paintings! Place a rainbow cutout in a lidded plastic container. Help each child dip marbles into colorful paint and then place them on the paper. Next, secure the lid and prompt the child to shake the container. Remove the lid to reveal a wacky and wonderful rainbow!

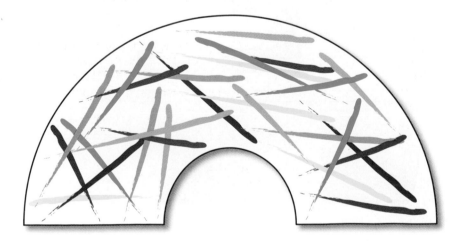

Snowy Day Relay

What is the best part of a snowy day? Playing in the snow, of course! Invite each child to put on a pair of mittens or gloves. Then divide the group into two teams and direct each team to form a line. Give the first child in each line a large polystyrene ball (snowball). On your signal, have each group pass the snowball down the line until it reaches the last person. Play several more rounds varying the way students pass the snowball each time.

Weather Window

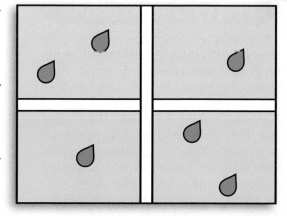

How should little ones dress when going outside? Encourage them to look out this special window to find out! Place felt strips on a flannelboard so it resembles a window. Provide felt weather-themed cutouts. Then stock the center with the suggested items. A child places desired cutouts on the window and then dresses to match the weather.

Suggested play items: coats and jackets of different weights, scarves, mittens, gloves, snow boots, rain boots, raincoats, rain hats, plastic ponchos, sunglasses, flip-flops, large short-sleeve shirts

Independent play

Watch It Rain

Little ones will delight in making their very own rainstorms. At the water table, place a selection of plastic containers, such as colanders, funnels, shaker bottles, plastic pitchers, watering cans, and squirt-style water bottles. Youngsters experiment with the different containers to create everything from a light sprinkle to a heavy downpour.

Brrrr!

Teacher-guided play

Fluffy Snowflakes

Review letter recognition with this fluffy snowflake play! Use a white crayon or gel pen to write letters on a large sheet of gray construction paper. Provide several cotton balls (snowflakes). Gather a small group of youngsters around the paper. Then name a letter and have a child use great dramatic flair to gently "float" a snowflake onto that letter. When the snowflake is in position, prompt students to hug themselves and say, "Brrrr!" Continue in the same way with different youngsters.

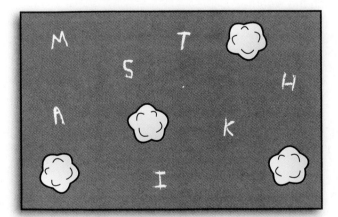

Windy Moves

How does the wind move things from place to place? Place the suggested items in your discovery area and let the windy investigation begin.

Suggested play items: straws (one per child), container of water, eye droppers, waxed paper, cotton balls, crumpled balls of paper, various sizes of pom-poms, crepe paper streamers, child-safe wind chime, pinwheel, craft feathers, fabric scraps

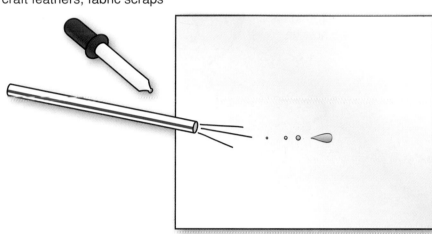

Puddle Play

Provide scissors and a variety of blue paper as well as a collection of stuffed toys. (Duck or frog stuffed toys may be particularly fun!) Little ones cut out puddle shapes and place them on the floor. Then they make the stuffed toys jump over, around, and into the puddles.

Wings

If I Had Wings...

Little ones' imaginations will soar with this entertaining oral-language activity. Invite each child to imagine he wakes up one morning to find he has wings. Encourage him to "fly" around his classmates and then tell them how he would use his new wings.

Busy Builders

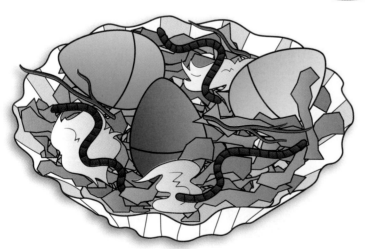

Preschoolers will fly over to the art center to build one of these unique nests. Set out glue and a variety of craft items, such as those suggested. Then let the creativity begin!

Suggested items: coffee filters, paper shreds, small leaf cutouts, paper scraps, cotton balls or batting, short lengths of yarn, twigs, raffia, craft feathers, small plastic eggs

Batty for B

Betty the bat needs the help of your little ones to clean out her cave. Prepare a bat puppet similar to the one shown (pattern on page 96). Then place a box on its side (cave). Put several objects with names that begin with /b/ in the cave along with a few distracter objects. Set a small empty trash can nearby. Have Betty explain to youngsters that she needs to clean her cave. Invite a volunteer to take an object from the cave and ask Betty if she wants to keep it. (Betty keeps the objects that begin with /b/.) If Betty wants to keep the object, have the child place it beside the cave; if not, have him place it in the trash can. Continue with the remaining objects.

Independent play

To the Bat Cave!

Create a reading area that your little ones will go batty over. Drape dark sheets or blankets over chairs to create a cave area large enough for two or three children. Stock the cave with fiction and nonfiction books about bats and provide a few flashlights. A cave visitor chooses a book and reads it by the light of the flashlight.

All About Bats

Silly Pigeon

Teacher-guided play

Little ones are sure to enjoy Pigeon's unwavering attempts to drive the bus in *Don't Let the Pigeon Drive the Bus!* by Mo Willems. After reading the story aloud, take on the role of Pigeon. Ask the group if you can do different activities. (Use activities a real pigeon would do along with some that it would not do.) After asking about an activity, direct the group to shout "yes" or "no," depending on whether the activity is something a real pigeon would do.

Wild Wings

Independent play

Youngsters work together to give this bird some stylish wings. Enlarge the bird pattern on page 96. Then make a copy for each child. Set out shallow containers of colorful paint and craft feathers. A child dips a feather into one color of paint and brushes it across the bird's wings. He continues with other colors of paint if desired.

Painted Beauties

What are brightly colored mirror images of each other? A butterfly's wings, of course! Show students several photos of butterflies and explain to them that a butterfly's wings are exactly alike. (If desired, use this opportunity to introduce the word *symmetry*.) Give each child a large butterfly cutout folded in half. Have her unfold the butterfly and use eyedroppers to drip paint on one wing. Then help her refold the butterfly, press on it, and unfold it again. Guide her to notice that the wings are identical. If desired, have her paint a body on her butterfly. Then display the butterflies around your classroom.

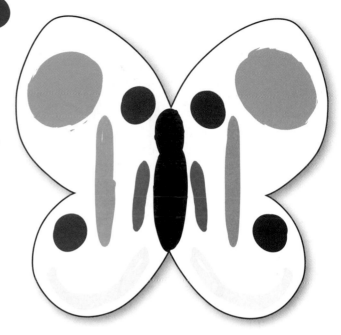

From Caterpillar to Butterfly

Little ones experience the life cycle of a butterfly during this adorable action poem.

I used to be an egg so tiny and round.
Then I was a caterpillar, crawling on the ground.
Next, I built a chrysalis and wrapped up tight.
I came out as a butterfly and then took flight!

Curl up into a ball.
Crawl on floor.
Wrap arms around self.
Flutter arms like wings.

Bird Pattern
Use with "Wild Wings" on page 94.

TEC61351

Bat Pattern
Use with "Batty for *B*" on page 93.

TEC61351